BETSY PENNINK

This is New York

HEINEMANN

BEGINNER LEVEL

Series Editor: John Milne

The Heinemann Guided Readers provide a choice of enjoyable reading material for learners of English. The series is published at five levels – Starter, Beginner, Elementary, Intermediate and Upper. At **Beginner Level**, the control of content and language has the following main features:

Information Control
The stories are written in a fluent and pleasing style with straightforward plots and a restricted number of main characters. The cultural background is made explicit through both words and illustrations. Information which is vital to the story is clearly presented and repeated where necessary.

Structure Control
Special care is taken with sentence length. Most sentences contain only one clause, though compound sentences are used occasionally with the clauses joined by the conjunctions 'and', 'but', and 'or'. The use of these compound sentences gives the text balance and rhythm. The use of Past Simple and Past Continuous Tenses is permitted since these are the basic tenses used in narration and students must become familiar with these as they continue to extend and develop their reading ability.

Vocabulary Control
At **Beginner Level** there is a controlled vocabulary of approximately 600 basic words, so that students with a basic knowledge of English will be able to read with understanding and enjoyment. Help is also given in the form of vivid illustrations which are closely related to the text.

For further information on the full selection of Readers at all five levels in the series, please refer to the Heinemann Readers catalogue.

CONTENTS

Introduction   4
1   History of New York   5
2   Getting to Know New York   10
3   Things to See and Do   19
4   Glossary of American/British
    English   30
5   Information and Advice   31

INTRODUCTION

New York is the biggest city in the United States of America. More than eight million people live and work in New York. Another ten million people live very near. Many of these people work in New York too.

New York is one of the most important cities in the world. It is a center for business. It is also a center for music and art.

New York is an exciting city. It has many famous buildings and places of interest. But New York is exciting because of its people. They come from many different countries of the world. Let us look at this unusual city.

Skyscrapers in New York

1 HISTORY of NEW YORK

The Indians and the Dutch

A Delaware Indian Chief

The first people in New York were American Indians. They lived on an island – Manhattan Island – at the beginning of a wide river. The island also had a beautiful harbor. The Indians killed animals and they sold the fur.

One day, in 1609, a ship came into the harbor. It was a Dutch ship and its captain was Henry Hudson. He saw the river and he sailed up it. He met the Indians and they sold him some fur.

Hudson returned to the Netherlands. He described the harbor and he showed the fur. After that, many Dutch ships went to Manhattan Island.

The Dutch men bought fur from the Indians. In 1626, one of the Dutch leaders bought Manhattan Island from the Indians. He gave them about twenty-four dollars.

New Amsterdam and New York

Fort nieuw Amsterdam op de Manhatans.

Map of New Amsterdam, 1628

Some Dutch people built small houses on Manhattan Island near the harbor. They called their little town New Amsterdam. Then other Europeans bought land from the Dutch and they built houses too. In 1643, about five hundred people lived in New Amsterdam. They spoke eighteen different languages. Most of them traded with the Indians.

At that time the English had land all around New Amsterdam. They wanted the town and the harbor too. They also wanted to buy more fur from the Indians. So one day, in 1664, an English ship went into the harbor. The Dutch quickly gave the little town to the English. New Amsterdam became New York and New York became a colony of England.

Independence

In 1755, the French and the English were fighting in North America. Both countries wanted more trade with the Indians. The war was won by the English in 1763.

After the war, the English needed money. Many ships went from England to the colonies in North America. Some carried glass. Others carried paper and tea. The English taxed these things. The people in New York had to pay the tax. And the tax made the people very angry.

People in the other English colonies became angry too. 'Why must we pay taxes to the government in England?' they asked. There was a war against the government of King George III of England.

The War of Independence: George Washington crossing the Delaware River, 1776

The War of Independence began in 1776. The Americans had a great leader – George Washington. He became General Washington. Later, he became the first President of the United States of America.

George Washington fought the English in New York City, but the English were very strong there. The English stayed in New York during the War of Independence. They finally left in 1783. New York City was the capital of the new country, the United States of America, for a year, 1789 to 1790.

The Immigrants

After the War of Independence, people came to America from all parts of the world. They wanted to live in the new country. They came by ship to New York. Some ships carried more than a thousand immigrants.

At first, people from England and Scotland arrived in New York. From 1840 to 1850 most of the immigrants

Ellis Island, New York, 1898. Immigrants left the ships and came here first

Immigrants arriving in New York, 1892

were German and Irish. During the next ten years, thousands of Italians landed in New York. Many Jewish people came at that time too.

By 1890, New York had more immigrants than any other city in the world. There were as many Germans in New York as in Hamburg. There were twice as many Irish people in New York as in Dublin. And every year more immigrants came. In one year – 1907 – 1 285 349 people arrived in New York.

Some of these immigrants went to other parts of the United States. But most of them stayed in New York.

There were many problems. The immigrants in New York had no money and they did not speak English. But usually immigrants from the same country lived close together. They helped each other. These new Americans worked very hard. Today New York has an interesting mixture of people and customs.

2 GETTING to KNOW NEW YORK

New York's Five Boroughs

Today, Manhattan Island is the center of New York. But Manhattan is only one part of the city. There are four other parts. These five parts are called boroughs.

The Bronx is the only borough on the mainland. All the other boroughs are on islands. There are many parks in the Bronx and the well-known baseball team – the New York Yankees – has its home there.

Brooklyn and Queens are on the west end of Long Island. Brooklyn became a borough of New York in 1898. Two and a half million people live there now. It has a famous beach – Coney Island – and a famous shipyard.

Queens is the largest borough. Many visitors to New York arrive in Queens. The John F. Kennedy International Airport is there.

Coney Island

A View of Brooklyn and Queens

Another borough – Staten Island – is at the beginning of New York Harbor. Not many people live on this large island. It has many lakes and trees. In 1964, the beautiful Verrazano Bridge was built between Brooklyn and Staten Island.

Manhattan is a long, narrow island. It goes north and south. The Hudson River is on the west of Manhattan. On the other side of the island is the East River. The Harlem River is between Manhattan and the Bronx.

There are fifteen bridges over the East River and the Harlem River. The George Washington Bridge is the only bridge over the Hudson River. It was built in 1931.

Getting Around in New York

Street signs in New York City

It is easy to find your way in Manhattan. Most streets go east and west. They do not have names. They have numbers. Most avenues go north and south. Some have names and some have numbers.

City crowds

Look at the map on pages 14 and 15. Central Park is in the middle of Manhattan. Can you find Fifth Avenue on the east side of Central Park? Everything to the east of Fifth Avenue is called the *East Side*. Everything to the west is the *West Side*.

The words *uptown, downtown* and *crosstown* are important in Manhattan. *Uptown* means north. *Downtown* means south. *Crosstown* means east or west.

New York has an underground railway. It is called the subway. There are many different subway lines in New York. In Manhattan, most of them go north and south.

All subway rides cost the same. A long ride does not cost more than a short one. First you buy a subway token. Then you pay for your ride with the token.

There are buses on most avenues in Manhattan. There are also buses on the large crosstown streets. You can pay for your bus ride with a subway token or with coins. But you must have the right coins. Bus drivers do not make change. All of the subways and most of the buses run twenty-four hours a day.

You can see taxis in New York very easily. They are usually yellow.

A yellow taxi

NEW YORK

1 Statue of Liberty
2 Empire State Building
3 United Nations
4 St Patrick's Cathedral
5 American Museum of Natural History
6 Guggenheim Museum
7 Yankee Stadium
8 Lincoln Center

HUDSON RIVER

TIMES SQUARE

MADISON SQUARE GARDEN

RADIO CITY MUSIC HALL

MET MUS

MUSEUM of MODERN ART

34TH STREET

FIFT

WORLD TRADE CENTER

GRAND CENTRAL STATION

LAFAYETTE STREET

CHINA TOWN

LITTLE ITALY

BOWERY

WALL STREET

STOCK EXCHANGE

STATEN ISLAND FERRY

LOWER EAST SIDE

BROOKLYN BRIDGE

MANHATTAN BRIDGE

TO CONEY ISLAND AND VERRAZANO NARROWS BRIDGE

BROOKLYN

TO BROOKLYN MUSEUM AND BROOKLYN BOTANIC GARDEN

EAST RIVER

14

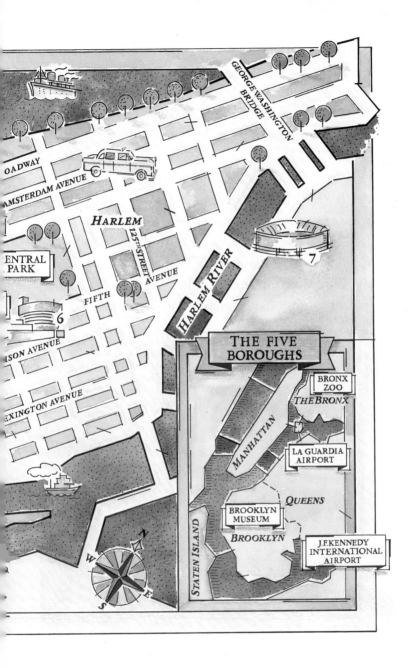

OADWAY

AMSTERDAM AVENUE

HARLEM

125TH STREET

AVENUE

CENTRAL
PARK

FIFTH

6

ISON AVENUE

LEXINGTON AVENUE

GEORGE WASHINGTON BRIDGE

HARLEM RIVER

7

N
W   E
S

**THE FIVE
BOROUGHS**

BRONX
ZOO

THE BRONX

LA GUARDIA
AIRPORT

MANHATTAN

QUEENS

STATEN ISLAND

BROOKLYN
MUSEUM

BROOKLYN

J.F. KENNEDY
INTERNATIONAL
AIRPORT

Neighborhoods

The streets of New Amsterdam were very narrow. Today the streets in the old part of New York are still narrow. But the buildings are very high. One of these narrow streets is *Wall Street*. It is the financial center of the United States. Many banks have offices there.

To the north of Wall Street is *Chinatown*. Mott Street is the main street of Chinatown. It is full of Chinese restaurants, vegetable markets and little shops. Many signs are in Chinese. People from China first came here in 1875. Now hundreds of Chinese live in the same old houses. More Chinese people want to live in Chinatown, but it is not big enough.

The Stock Exchange in Wall Street

Shops and signs in Chinatown

Little Italy is north of Chinatown between Lafayette Street and the Bowery. Between 1890 and 1924, about four million Italians arrived in New York. Many of them found homes in the old houses in Little Italy. This is still a center for Italian people in New York. Every September, a big Italian celebration – the San Gennaro Festival – takes place here.

By 1915, there were 1 400 000 Jews in New York. Many of them came from Eastern Europe and they lived together in the *Lower East Side*. They made clothes in their homes and sold them. Today Jewish shops on Orchard Street sell all kinds of clothes. They are much cheaper than in the big stores. But Jewish people do not work on Saturdays, so Sunday is a very busy day in the Lower East Side.

After 1918, many black people in the south of the United States moved to New York. They lived in *Harlem*, north of Central Park. They brought their customs and their music from the South. Harlem became famous for its jazz music.

125th Street is the main shopping street in Harlem. In some parts of Harlem, the buildings are very bad, but there are also new houses and apartments.

Spanish Harlem is east of Black Harlem. Many Puerto Ricans live there. In the streets, Spanish is spoken and the signs over the shops are in Spanish too.

Singers and musicians in Harlem

3 THINGS to SEE and DO

Manhattan and Central Park

The Skyscrapers

Everyone has seen pictures of the high buildings in Manhattan. These very high buildings are called skyscrapers.

From 1931 to 1970, the highest building in the world was the *Empire State Building*. It is 102 stories high and there is a very good view of the city from the top.

Now the *World Trade Center* is higher than the Empire State Building. The two buildings of the World Trade Center are the highest buildings in New York. Visitors can see the city and the harbor from the top of one of these buildings.

19

The Statue of Liberty

A boat ride on the river

Boat Rides

The *Statue of Liberty* stands on a small island in New York Harbor. She was a gift from the French in 1886. The Statue looks towards the entrance to the harbor. She is welcoming immigrants to America.

Boats take visitors from Manhattan Island to the Statue of Liberty. There are stairs inside the Statue. Visitors can walk up the stairs to the head of the Statue. They look out from there at the harbor.

There are also boat trips around *Manhattan Island*. Each trip takes about three hours. A guide tells about the buildings, the rivers and the bridges during the ride.

The United Nations

The *United Nations* headquarters is on the East River between 42nd Street and 48th Street. In 1952, there were 51 flags at the front of the buildings. There was one flag for each member of the United Nations. Now there are 166 flags for the 166 members.

Visitors can take an interesting tour through the buildings. They can also get tickets for a meeting of the General Assembly. The meetings of the General Assembly usually start in September every year.

The United Nations headquarters

Rockefeller Center

There are twenty-one buildings in *Rockefeller Center* on Fifth Avenue. It is a beautifully designed office center and visitors admire its small garden and skating rink.

One well-known building is *Radio City Music Hall*. Six thousand people can see a show on the big stage. The Rockettes – a famous dancing group of thirty girls – dance in this show.

Radio City at night

St Patrick's Cathedral

St Patrick's Cathedral is across Fifth Avenue from Rockefeller Center. The Cathedral was built in 1879. At that time, many rich people moved to apartments on Fifth Avenue. St Patrick's Cathedral became the center of the *Easter Parade*.

The Easter Parade is not a parade with soldiers. Anybody can be in the parade. On Easter Sunday many people go to church in the Cathedral and the churches near there. They wear their best clothes. After church everyone walks or parades up and down Fifth Avenue.

St Patrick's Cathedral

Shopping

Macy's – the largest department store

Fifth Avenue is New York's most famous shopping street. The best stores are between 34th Street and 58th Street. Some are very large and well-known. Many people shop for clothes at *B. Altman, Lord and Taylor* and *Saks Fifth Avenue. Tiffany and Company* is the best-known jewelry store. It is also famous for its silver.

Almost every avenue in Manhattan has stores. Most of the stores on Madison Avenue are small boutiques. Many shops on Third Avenue sell antiques.

Macy's on 34th Street is the largest department store in New York. It is known for its low prices, but nothing is very cheap today!

24

New York's Parks

Central Park in Manhattan is used by thousands of New Yorkers and visitors every day. Many of them like to walk in the Park. Others like to ice-skate or go to the Zoo.

In summer, lots of people go out in boats on the Lake. Horses pull carriages through the Park.

On summer evenings, there are outdoor concerts in the Park. Many of Shakespeare's plays are performed there too.

New York's most important zoo is in the Bronx. The *Bronx Zoo* is the largest zoo in America. It is also very modern. Many animals are not in cages. They can walk around in grass and climb trees. There is only water between the animals and the visitors.

Ice-skating in Central Park

Museums

The most famous art museum in New York is the *Metropolitan Museum of Art*. The Museum is in Central Park on Fifth Avenue. It has great collections from all over the world. It also has a concert hall.

In Manhattan, two other art museums are the *Museum of Modern Art* and the *Guggenheim Museum*. The Guggenheim Museum is an unusual, round building. In Brooklyn, there is another great museum, the *Brooklyn Museum*.

The *American Museum of Natural History* is on the west side of Central Park in Manhattan. It is an important science museum.

The Guggenheim Museum

Fast food – a hot dog stand

Restaurants

There are thousands of restaurants in New York. They serve every kind of food in the world.

Most restaurants in Chinatown are Chinese. There are many Italian restaurants in Little Italy and many German restaurants around East 86th Street.

Many New Yorkers do not have much time for lunch. They eat in 'fast food' places. They sit at a counter and have hamburgers and coffee. Or they buy food from stands like the one above. Sometimes they carry the food to their offices and eat it there.

Entertainment

Broadway is famous for its theaters. One part of Broadway is sometimes called The Great White Way. The lights from all the theaters and advertisements here are very bright. There are more than thirty theaters in this district.

Times Square is the center of the theater district. An important evening in Times Square is New Year's Eve – 31st December. Crowds of people stand in the Square and wait for midnight. At midnight, everyone shouts "Happy New Year!" to everyone else.

Times Square at night

Lincoln Center

There are small theaters in other parts of New York. These are called Off-Broadway theaters. New and unusual plays are performed there.

Movie theaters are everywhere in New York. Magazines give the names and the times of the films.

Opera, ballet and concerts are performed at *Lincoln Center*. The buildings are modern and Chagall's paintings in the *Metropolitan Opera House* are very beautiful. Lincoln Center is on Broadway at 64th Street.

The new *Madison Square Garden* was built in 1968. Many kinds of sports events take place there. Once a year, the biggest circus in the world comes there too.

4 GLOSSARY of AMERICAN/ BRITISH ENGLISH

Some words are spelt differently in American and British English. These are a few of them.

American English	British English
center	centre
harbor	harbour
neighborhood	neighbourhood
theater	theatre

Other words are different in American and British English.

American English	British English
apartment	flat
make change	give change
movie	film
movie theater	cinema
subway	underground railway/ tube

5 INFORMATION and ADVICE

Perhaps you will visit New York one day. You might be a student there. Here is some advice. Get a good map of the city. It will also have subway and bus maps. Remember the directions – uptown and downtown, east and west. Feel the excitement of New York. Have fun!

General Information

Tourist Offices

New York Convention and
  Visitors' Bureau
2 Columbus Circle
New York, NY 10019
Telephone (212) 397–8222

Times Square Information
  Center
42nd Street and Times
  Square
Telephone (212) 397–8222
Travelers' Aid Society
158 W 42nd Street
New York, NY 10036
Telephone (212) 944–0013

Transport Information

New York Subways and
  Buses
Telephone (718) 330–1234

Useful Phone Numbers

The weather (212) 976–1212
The time (212) 976–1616
Emergency:
  Police, Fire, Ambulance 911
  or 'O' for Operator

Magazines/Books

Seeing New York:
The official MTA Travel Guide
published by the
Metropolitan Transportation
Authority

Heinemann English Language Teaching
Halley Court, Jordan Hill, Oxford OX2 8EJ
A division of Reed Educational & Professional Publishing Limited

OXFORD MADRID FLORENCE ATHENS PRAGUE
SÃO PAULO MEXICO CITY CHICAGO PORTSMOUTH(NH)
TOKYO SINGAPORE KUALA LUMPUR MELBOURNE
AUCKLAND JOHANNESBURG IBADAN GABORONE

Heinemann is a registered trademark of Reed Educational & Professional
Publishing Limited

ISBN 0 435 27178 4

A recorded version of this story is available on cassette.
ISBN 0 435 27285 3

Acknowledgements
The authors and publishers would like to thank the following for permission to
reproduce their photographs and artwork: Reproduced by permission of the
American Museum in Britain, Bath p5; Michael Boyd p13 (br); Bridgeman Art
Library/Metropolitan Museum of Art, New York p7; Colorific!/Black Star/Joseph
Rodriguez p18; Greg Evans Photo Library p24; Mary Evans Picture Library p6;
Susan Griggs Agency/Richard Laird p20 (b); Image Bank/Grant V Faint p12; Image
Bank/Marc Romanelli p13 (c); Impact Photos/Martin Black p17; The Mansell
Collection p8, p9; Photographers Library p25; Jan Quantrill p11; Visionbank
Library Ltd, London p10; Tony Stone Photo Library p4; Tony Stone Photo Lib-
rary/Doug Armand p16, p22, p26; Tony Stone Photo Library/Joseph Poberestein
p19; Tony Stone Photo Library/Jon Riley p21; Tony Stone Photo Library/Rohan
p20 (t); Zefa p27; Zefa/H. Steenmans p23.

Typography by Adrian Hodgkins
Cover by David Sim and Threefold Design
Map by Sue Potter
Typeset in 12/16 pt Goudy
by Joshua Associates Ltd, Oxford
Printed and bound in Malta by Interprint Limited

97 98 99 00 01 10 9 8 7